50 Wonderful Word Games

Easy and Entertaining Activities That Build Essential Language-Arts Skills

by Alan Trussell-Cullen

SCHOLASTIC
PROFESSIONAL BOOKS

New York ■ Toronto □ London ■ Auckland □ Sydney

Dedicated to the best word gamesters and word game guinea pigs I know—my family!

Cheers!

- Alan

Cover design by Jaime Lucero
Cover illustration by Anna Walker
Interior design by Jaime Lucero and Liza Charlesworth for Grafica, Inc.
Interior illustrations by Chris Reed

ISBN 0-590-96559-X

Table of Contents

Introduction

Playing games is fundamental to human behavior. It's in our genes! Even babies play games. One of their favorites is "Drop the Rattle Out of the Crib and See How Many Times You Can Make Your Parents Pick It Up!" Then there's "How Much of the Living Room Floor Can I Cover With My Blocks and Toys?" Of course, when they get older they play other games, like "How Many Times Can I Get My Parents to Ask Me to Do Something Without My Actually Getting Around to Doing It?"

The truth of the matter is that we all play games. It's how we explore the world and find out who we are.

Games are fun, too, and some of the most enjoyable and creative games are the ones we play with words. The wonderful thing is that they can also be powerful learning tools.

Playing word games is a great way to get to know new people and become comfortable with new surroundings—a new class, a new teacher, or a new school. Chapter One has some wonderful getting-to-know-you games that help with this. Word games can also help develop oral language, and Chapter Two features great games for developing our speaking and listening skills. In addition to using words when we speak, we write them, too. We can make patterns with them and play games with those patterns. Chapter Three has some great games for word-doodling (and, thus, mind-doodling).

Word games can improve our writing, too. They can help us with spelling and grammar skills, punctuation, and creativity. Maybe writing is a game anyway. Don't we tempt and tease our readers, sometimes surprising them and sometimes reassuring them? Sometimes we strut with our words. Sometimes we inform with our words—or shock or show off or even hide behind our words. The word games in Chapter Four can hone the skills we need to do all of this.

Still, words are much more than the letters we print on a page or the recognizable speech sounds we cluster together and let tumble from our lips. Words encode ideas. Games can help us experiment with ideas, categorize them, find similarities and differences, grid them, dramatize them, combine them with other ideas, and hammer

them into brand-new ideas. In Chapter Five we look at brain-stretching word games that do all this and more. Throughout this book we have also included under the heading Try This! additional language arts activities and projects that develop vocabulary and build skills.

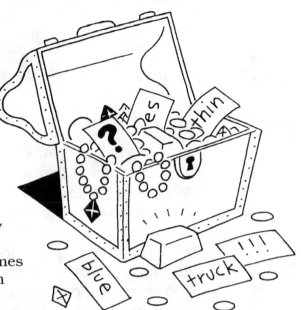

So the word games in this book assist with many important learning skills. We may choose to play them for those reasons, or we may play word games simply for the pleasure they bring to our children and the joy they spread in our classrooms.

Beyond their fun and linguistic value, word games contribute to much more complex and important parts of our education. They teach us about life. They offer that wonderful combination of freedom and responsibility—the chance to be creative and take risks while obeying the rules.

The fact that games are enjoyable and even somewhat addictive may bring another powerful and perhaps more pervasive benefit to our classrooms. If our children really enjoy playing a game, they won't just play it at school. They'll play it whenever they have spare time and wherever they happen to be—at school or at home. In other words, they'll continue to practice the skills implicit in the game long after the classroom session is over.

Think of it! They'll be learning when they don't even know they're learning. They might become so excited about these games that they turn off the TV and tune in instead to the people and the world around them. This could prove to be the start of a revolution!

Happy word-game playing!

Words!

Words—
Hear them! Say them!
Think them! Play them!
Whisper them! Exclaim them!
Conceal them! Proclaim them!
Words—
Murmur them, mumble them,
Burble them, jumble them
Sing them and shout them
Just daydream about them
Words—
Taste them, smell them
Scribble them, spell them
Savor and relish them
Adorn them, embellish them
Adapt them, invent them,
Change what is meant by them
Words—
Act them, mime them
Rhythm and rhyme them
Print them, type them
Holler and hype them
Match and marry them
Cash and carry them
Words—
They're treasure-trove and plunderful
They're hip hooray and fun-for-all
They're rag-bag and blunderful
They're mind blown-asunder-ful
They're lightning and thunderful!
Yes
I guess
Words are just wonderful!

–Alan Trussell-Cullen

Name Chants

☆ About the Game

This activity makes it easy for children to get to know one another's names and feel comfortable as a group.

☆ How-To's

1. Everyone sits facing inward in a circle. It's a good idea for you to take part in order to model the actions.

2. Explain that all of you are going to introduce yourselves by name. (Children can use first names. You may do the same or use Ms./Mr. and your last name.)

3. Begin by setting up this pattern of activity: Slowly, clap your hands twice, pat your knees twice, and then extend your hands twice in a giving gesture (palms up), at the same time chanting your name (for example, Jennifer! Jennifer! or Ms. Adams! Ms. Adams!).

4. The class now repeats the whole pattern with you, including the chant of your name.

5. The next child in the circle now goes through the pattern, chanting his or her name (Clap! Clap! Knees! Knees! Hands/Name! Hands/Name!), and then everyone repeats it. And so it continues around the circle.

6. When the name-chanting has gone full circle, you start again. This time, however, you only do the two claps and two knee-taps to establish the rhythm. Everyone else follows, chanting each person's name in turn: Clap! Clap! Knees! Knees! Jennifer! Jennifer! David! David! William! William! Josh! Josh! Linda! Linda!, etc.

Skills: Develops self-confidence, social skills, and class rapport.

Players: Large group or whole class.

Materials: None.

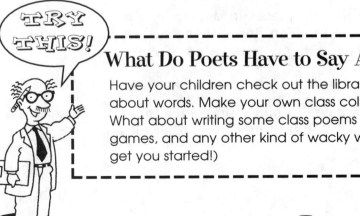

TRY THIS!

What Do Poets Have to Say About Words?

Have your children check out the library or media center to find poems about words. Make your own class collection called Poems About Words. What about writing some class poems about word play, word fun, word games, and any other kind of wacky wordery? (The poem on page 6 can get you started!)

Silent Circles

☆ About the Game

This is a word game that is played without words! The main value of the game—apart from the fun of playing it—is that it encourages children to appreciate why we have words and how we use them.

☆ How-To's

1. Begin by explaining that the children are going to form a special kind of birthday circle. Children arrange themselves in a circle in which everyone in front of them will have a birthday that comes earlier in the year than theirs and everyone behind them will have a birthday that comes later in the year. For example, a child with a birthday of June 2 might have someone with a birthday of May 28 in front of him and someone with a birthday of June 15 behind him.

2. Of course, because this is a circle, it won't have a start or a finish. A child who has a birthday in December (or the end of the year) will come before a child who has a birthday in January (or the start of the year).

3. To form the circle, children have to find out everyone else's birthday. However—and this is the important rule—they must do it without speaking. They can use sign language, frame letters and numbers with their hands, or even use their fingers to write a month or number on the back of someone else's hand. It's up to the children to decide the best strategy.

4. You may find it a good idea to join in the game. You can model some of the strategies if children seem to be stuck. (In that case, of course, you aren't allowed to speak, either!)

5. After all the children have found their places in the circle, a good way to complete the game is for the children to all sit down at the same time. The child with the first birthday in the year can give some kind of signal.

☆ Variations

Instead of birthdays, try forming circles based on some other form of personal data, such as alphabetical order of first names. Any other ideas?

TRY THIS!

Friendly Greetings from Around the World

- ■ Start a collection called Greetings from Around the World.

- ❑ Have children write the greetings in speech bubbles and pin them on the appropriate country (or countries) on a map of the world.

- ■ In addition to formal greetings ("Good morning," "Bonjour"), include some informal ones, too ("Hi"—USA; "How's it going, Mate?"—Australia; "Top of the morning to you"—Ireland).

- ❑ Encourage children to use the greetings with one another.

- ■ Model them yourself—when taking attendance, for example.

- ❑ Help children find out more about the country in which the greetings are used and the people who use them.

Some Greetings to Start Your Collection

Hello	USA, UK, Canada, Australia, New Zealand
Apa kabar [AH-pah KAH-bar]	Indonesia
Ciao [chow]	Italy
Salut [sah-LEW]	France
Bonjour [bone-JOOR]	
Tag, wie geht's? [TAHG, vee-GETS]	Germany
Hola [OH-lah]	Spain, Mexico
Kia ora [KEE-ah OH-rah]	Maori, New Zealand
Chao [chow]	Vietnam
Goede dag [GOO-tuh DAHG]	Netherlands
Goddag [god-DAH]	Denmark
Szervusz [SAIR-voos]	Hungary

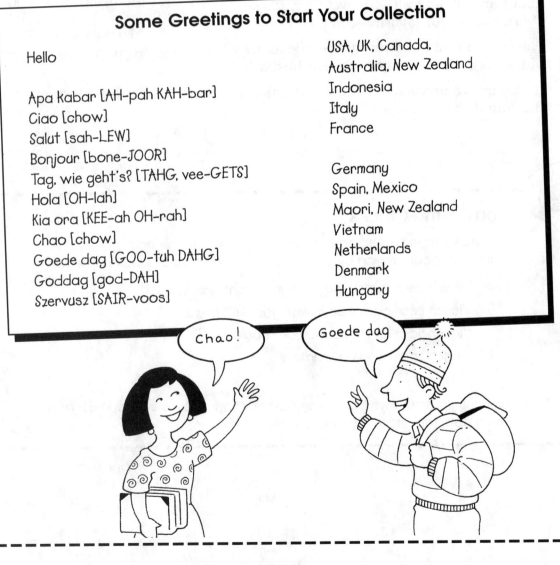

No, Yes! No, No!

 ## About the Game

This game is an old favorite. Players have to listen carefully and be thoughtful about what they say. It's also a good getting-to-know-you game.

How-To's

1. Either divide the class into pairs or have pairs play in turn in front of the class.

2. Player One asks Player Two ten questions about anything at all—the weather, Player Two's hobbies or favorite foods, etc.

3. Player Two must answer all the questions without saying yes or no and without hesitating.

4. If Player Two answers all the questions according to the rules, he or she wins the round. If not, Player One wins.

Skills: Develops concentration, self-confidence, social skills, and listening skills.

Players: Pairs (though it is a fun spectator game for the rest of the class).

Materials: None.

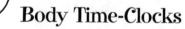

Body Time-Clocks

In games where players have to do something without hesitating, settle arguments about timing by using the five-second body-clock as follows:

Touch your left elbow with your right hand.

Touch your right elbow with your left hand.

Touch your hands behind your back.

Touch your hands in front.

Time's up!

Try inventing your own body time-clock actions—for example, cross arms, touch ears, tap knees, etc. Have fun!

Hink Pinks

☆ About the Game

A great game for encouraging children to play with language—to try out new vocabulary, embellish descriptions, practice writing definitions, and above all enjoy the power words have over the world around us.

☆ How-To's

1. One child thinks of a noun (it could be a part of the body, like a finger; an object, like a shoe; or an animal, like a cat or pig) and an adjective that rhymes with it. For example, a "hink pink," a "blue shoe," a "fat cat," a "big pig," or a "wary canary."

2. The child then makes up an elaborate definition of the rhyming object. Here are a few examples to share with your class: an ink-stained little finger for an "inky pinky"; a sky-colored object you keep your feet in for a "blue shoe"; an overfed feline for a "fat cat"; an enormous lump of living ham for a "big pig"; a cautious caged bird of yellow hue for a "wary canary."

3. The other players now have to guess what the object is.

☆ Variation

Encourage children to write their Hink Pinks definitions on a class Hink Pinks Display Board. Other children can write their answers on a piece of paper and pin them up alongside the definitions. Later on, the inventor can check them out and announce the real answer. You might encourage children to publish their own books of Hink Pinks (with the answers on the back page).

Skills: Develops vocabulary, use of grammar terms like noun and adjective, and publishing skills.

Players: Pairs, groups, or whole class.

Materials: None.

TRY THIS!

Words Travel!

Discuss with your children the great number of English words that have been "borrowed" from other languages, and then send them on a Word-Detective Hunt! They might like to start with these words and see if they can find out which language (and what part of the world) they came from.

pajama   taboo   ballet   muesli   balcony   schooner   yacht

Get children to help you find more words borrowed from other languages, and add them to the list. Put up a map of the world, and see if children can find enough borrowed words in the English language to take them around the world.

Where's the Rutabaga?

☆ About the Game

"Where's the Rutabaga?" is a tantalizing memory game, but above all it's a great opportunity to romp with words and ideas.

☆ How-To's

1. In this game, a player is asked a lot of simple questions—but has to remember all of his or her answers!

2. One player is chosen for questioning. The other players put their heads together to come up with a suitable opening question such as "Where's the rutabaga?"

3. They now chant the question at the player, who can make up any plausible answer. Then, the questioners turn the reply into another question, and so it goes on, as in the following exchange:

   Questioners: Where's the rutabaga?
   Player: In the fridge.
   Questioners: But where's the fridge?
   Player: In the kitchen.
   Questioners: But where's the kitchen?
   Player: In the house.

4. This continues until the questioners decide it's time to test the player's memory. They then spring the original question on the player—in this case, "Where's the rutabaga?" Now the player has to be able to run back through all the responses given so far, in reverse order:

   Questioners: Where's the rutabaga?
   Player: In the house, in the kitchen, in the fridge.

5. After children have played the game a few times, the excitement mounts as they wait for the memory test!

6. Of course, the game would become very predictable if it always started with the question, "Where's the rutabaga?" So the questioners need to dream up something different each time. This can be a lot of fun, too.

Skills: Develops memorization skills, ability to concentrate and generate ideas in logical sequence, familiarity with sets and subsets in mathematics, social skills, and class rapport.

Players: Pairs, or, better, large groups of up to 12.

Materials: None.

Knock! Knock!

☆ About the Game

This is a simple pun-fun game that most people have played at some time. Besides the laughter it can create, it has the educational merit of encouraging children to play with words. It can be an interesting class publishing project, too. Children can collect all the knock-knock jokes they can muster and compile a class book.

☆ How-To's

1. In advance have children collect (and write down) examples of knock-knock jokes. Encourage them to check out the library and ask friends and relatives. Better still, suggest that they make up jokes of their own.

2. When they have a good store of jokes, the game can begin! One player starts by declaring "Knock! Knock! . . ."

3. Another player answers "Who's there?"

4. Player One may now come up with something like "Don Giovanni!"

5. Player Two has to say "Don Giovanni who?"

6. Player One now says, "Don Giovanni ice cream today?" (Don't you have any ice cream today?)

At this point, everyone groans and someone else starts up with "Knock! Knock!. . ." Here are some more examples to start the ball rolling:

Skills: Listening skills, word study, and publishing skills.

Players: Pairs, but it works best when there is an audience to enjoy the puns.

Materials: None.

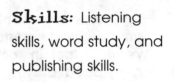

Some Knock-Knocks to Start Your Class Collection

Isabel.
Isabel who?
Isabel necessary on a bike?

Orange.
Orange who?
Orange you glad you asked?

Abigail.
Abigail who?
Abigail blew my house over!

Major.
Major who?
Major answer the door, didn't I?

Crambo

☆ About the Game

This game is certainly an old favorite. It's been amusing and entertaining people for hundreds of years. In fact, in 1660 Samuel Pepys wrote in his diary about playing Crambo on a horse-drawn coach ride.

☆ How-To's

1. One player thinks of a secret word (let's say it is *hand*) and writes it down on a piece of paper.

2. The player then thinks of a word that rhymes with the secret word (for example, *band*) and announces to the group, I hear, with my Crambo ear, something that rhymes with. . . band!

3. The player now asks the other children in the group what they think the Crambo word is.

4. The child who guesses correctly gets to think of the next Crambo word.

Skills: Listening skills and phonic awareness.

Players: Groups of four to eight.

Materials: Writing materials.

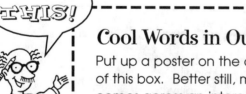

TRY THIS!

Cool Words in Our Classroom

Put up a poster on the classroom wall with a heading like the title of this box. Better still, make up your own. When a child uses or comes across an interesting or unusual word, make a fuss about it—and then write it on the poster. Better still, use the word and make a stupendous fuss when one of your children uses it!

Tongue Twisters

☆ About the Game

Nothing could be simpler than this game. Yet when children become acquainted with it, they go back to it again and again.

☆ How-To's

1. Appoint one child Timekeeper and another as the first player.

2. The group decides on a tongue twister, and, then the player is allowed to say it slowly twice—just to get his or her tongue into training.

3. Then the Timekeeper calls "Go!" and the player has to say the tongue twister as many times as possible in one minute. The rest of the group counts how many times the awkward utterance is completed correctly.

4. After one minute, the Timekeeper calls out "Stop!" and the listeners declare the score—the number of times the player said the complete tongue twister correctly.

5. A new challenger for the tongue-gymnastics title steps forward, and so the game goes on. (It sounds like a contest, but the real fun is in listening to what people say when their tongue refuses to wrap itself around the right words!)

Skills: Oral language skills, especially enunciation and listening skills (carefull listening to pick up the telltale slips of the tongue!).

Players: Any number from two to the whole class—a good audience game.

Materials: None.

Some Tongue Twisters to Start Your Class Collection

The sixth sheik's sixth sheep's sick.

Such pranks Frank's prawns play in the tank.

Some shun sunshine.

What noise annoys a noisy oyster? A noisy noise annoys a noisy oyster.

More Tongue Twisters for Your Class Collection

■ How much wood would a wood chuck chuck
   if a wood chuck could chuck wood?

☐ Peter Piper picked a peck of pickled peppers;
   A peck of pickled peppers Peter Piper picked;
   If Peter Piper picked a peck of pickled peppers,
   How many pickled peppers did Peter Piper pick?

■ Lemon liniment.

☐ A tutor who tooted the flute
   Tried to tutor two tooters to toot.
   Said the two to the tutor:
   Is it harder to toot or
   To tutor two tooters to toot?

■ She sells seashells by the seashore,
   The shells she sells are seashells, I'm sure,
   For if she sells seashells by the seashore,
   Then I'm sure she sells seashore shells.

Travelers' Tales

☆ About the Game

This is another good game for encouraging children to listen to letter sounds and learn their alphabet, while at the same time improving their skills with reference tools such as dictionaries and atlases. They may also pick up some geography along the way.

☆ How-To's

1. Write on the chalkboard or on large cards the following questions and a model answer:

   (Example: Letter C)

   Where are *you* going?
   I'm going to Chicago.
                (proper noun)

   What will *you* do there?
   Catch   some   crazy   cats.
   (verb)   **(adjective) (noun)**

Skills: Alphabet, dictionary, and atlas skills; phonic awareness; and grammar skills (revision of nouns, proper nouns, adjectives, and verbs).

Players: Large groups or whole class.

Materials: Pencil, paper, dictionary, and atlas or world map.

2. Use the following method to give everyone in the group a letter of the alphabet. Choose one child—let's say his name is Miguel. Let him keep the letter *m*, and then go around the rest of the class assigning each child a letter of the alphabet starting from *n*. (You may wish to omit such letters as *q*, *x*, and *z*.) When you reach the end of the alphabet, start over with *a* until everyone has a letter.

3. Children have to come up with answers that use their assigned letter. They can consult the atlas (or world map) and dictionary to help them.

4. When everyone has finished, the whole group asks each child in turn (in this case, starting with Miguel), "Where are you going?" Miguel may answer, "Mexico."

5. The group then asks, "What will you do there?"

   Miguel: Munch lots of marvelous melons!

☆ Variation

Have children cut out their written responses and pin them onto the appropriate place on the world map for others to read. After children have played the game two or three times, the world map becomes a center of great interest.

TRY THIS!

Savoring Words

Some words are just plain delicious to say. Saying them is a tactile experience! Talk about this with children. Share your own favorite words, and encourage them to start a class list of Great Words to Say.

Here are a few of my favorites:

flimsy

quip (and just about every other word that starts with Q)

appendectomy

filch

spindle

fickle

freckle

sizzle

salami

spaghetti

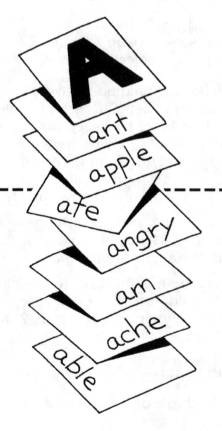

Rhyming Ketchup

☆ About the Game

You can set up this game quickly and keep it going for as long a time as you wish.

☆ How-To's

1. Players sit in a circle facing inward. The player holding the ball begins by saying a one-syllable word, such as *red*.

2. The ball is then handed (not thrown!) to the next player, who has to say a word that rhymes with the first one—for example, *bed*.

3. The ball is passed to the next player for another rhyme, and so on.

4. Only the first word needs to be a one-syllable word. After that, players can use as many syllables as they like—for example, *forehead*, or *interpreted*!

5. Players have to come up with the rhyming word the moment the object is handed to them. If a player can't think of one, or fails to say it at once, the rest of the group looks at him or her and says (kindly) "Oh! Ketchup!"

6. The player is now allowed to start a new round. This time they might begin with *hot* or *fun* or. . . .

Skills: Listening skills, concentration, social skills, and rhyming skills.

Players: Any number from four to the whole class.

Materials: a Tennis ball (or other object) to pass around the group and dictionary (to check out any words under dispute).

TRY THIS!

Word of the Day

Each day, choose one word that you want to give VIW (Very Important Word) status. It might be a word related to something the class is studying at the moment or to an experience the children have had recently. Write it in big letters on the chalkboard, along with a definition, a sentence in which it's used, and some clues as to how to pronounce it.

Our Word of the Day: Motivate

To make someone very keen to do something.
"She likes watching runners on TV because it can motivate her to work even harder at her own training."

How to say it: MOH-ti-vate.

Mystery Letters

☆ **About the Game**

This is a great game that helps children focus on letter sounds!

☆ **How-To's**

1. One player starts the game by choosing a mystery letter.

2. That player then goes up to the other players one at a time and asks a question that requires a one- or two-word answer, as in the following example:

   Player: Rachel, how old are you?

   Player: Ten.

3. If the answer contains the mystery letter, the player responds, "That's terrific!" If it doesn't, the response is "That's terrible!"

   If the mystery letter is *m*, the game might go on like this:

   Player: Uma, do you live in the town or the country?

   Uma: The country.

   Player: That's terrible! Ranjit, what time did you have breakfast today?

   Ranjit: Eight.

   Player: That's terrible! Anna, what is your favorite drink?

   Anna: Milk.

   Player: That's terrific! Whitney, what would you like to get for your birthday?

   Whitney: A camcorder.

   Player: That's terrific!

4. The game continues until someone guesses the mystery letter.

Skills: Listening skills, spelling skills, and phonic awareness.

Players: Any number from two to the whole class.

Materials: None.

Mum's the Word

☆ About the Game

This is an "elimination" game that children can play anywhere—at school, on a bus, at home with the family, even at parties.

☆ How-To's

1. Together, the class picks a small word that is used frequently in conversation—such as *the*, *and*, *that*, or *only*. This is declared to be the "mum" word, a word no one can speak.

2. One child is chosen to be the Mum's the Word tester. He or she goes around the group asking questions and trying to trick the other players into saying the forbidden word. Any player who does say it drops out. The game continues until there is one "winner" left.

To the victorious class member who successfully refrained from using <u>the</u> , <u>that</u>, <u>only</u>, & <u>and</u>.

Never-Ending Sentences

☆ About the Game

Children work together to keep a single sentence growing and growing, so this game's great for fostering collaborative work skills and attitudes. It's also the kind of game you can play anywhere (on a long bus ride) or anytime (when the class finishes a task early and there are a few minutes to spare).

☆ How-To's

1. One child sets the game in motion by saying a word that could come at the start of a sentence. For example: "Once ..."

2. Player One now points to another player, who has to say the next word in this group-generated sentence: "...upon..."

3. Player Two points to someone else, who has to carry on from there: "...a..."

4. And so the game goes on until the current player thinks the sentence has gone on long enough or can't think of a way of continuing it. He or she then declares, "And they all lived happily ever after!"

5. Now another player is chosen to start a new sentence.

Skills: Listening skills, concentration, sentence-building skills, and social skills.

Players: Any number from six to the whole class.

Materials: None.

Toppers

☆ About the Game

This is a lively word-play and language-stretching game. It may turn your class into the world's best exaggerators!

☆ How-To's

1. First, the group decides on a quality or an action (see below for some suggestions). Let's say the group decides on the action "snores so loudly."

2. The first player, Patty, invents a fictitious relative or other character. Let's say she chooses an Aunty Flo: "My Aunty Flo snores so loudly that pictures fall off the wall!"

3. She now chooses Dave as the next player, and he has to try to "top" her story: "My Uncle Don snores so loudly that he keeps himself awake!"

4. The next player says "My Cousin Jim snores so loudly that the people next door put up their storm windows!"

5. The players continue until someone gets stuck or everyone is laughing too much. Then the group chooses a new quality or action, and the game goes on.

Yeehaw!

TRY THIS!

Some Toppers to Get You Started

snores so loudly	is so generous	runs so fast
eats so slowly	grows cabbages so big	laughs so oddly
is so clumsy	is so untidy	is so noisy
is so forgetful	is so smart	is so mean

Word Ladders

☆ About the Game

Lewis Carroll is credited with inventing this game. Maybe that's why it seems to take you into an Alice's Wonderland where cats can turn into dogs, work into play, and morning into evening!

☆ How-To's

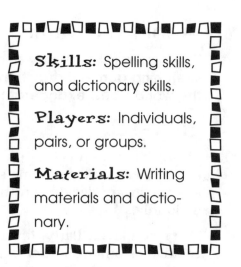

1. If playing on their own, children start with two words that have the same number of letters. (You may assign the words, or children may choose their own.) One word is the top of the ladder, where they start, and the other is the bottom of the ladder, where they hope to end up. How about *cat* and *dog*?

2. Children try to think of a word that differs by one letter from the top word. If possible, the new letter should be in the bottom-rung word: for example, *cot*. (With some words, especially longer ones, this direct route may not be possible. So it's a good idea to use tested words.)

3. Children change one letter at a time. Each change must make a real word:

CAT   COT   COG   DOG

4. Some other examples include turning a HAND into a FOOT:

HAND   HIND   FIND   FOND   FONT   FOOT

5. You can also turn the MOON into a STAR:

MOON   LOON   LOOK   BOOK   BOOT   BOAT

BOAR   SOAR   STAR

6. For the group version of Word Ladders, assign the same starting and finishing words to all groups. Children in each group work together to see who can be first to complete the word ladder.

☆ Tip:
Start with words of only three or four letters. You don't have to finish word ladder in one sitting. Set some word-ladder pairs as puzzles, and see if the children can solve them in their spare time. A challenging word ladder might take days to complete—or prove impossible! You might have children contribute their word ladders to a class book. Also encourage them to play this game at home with their friends and families. Want some examples to start with? Try turning *flour* into *bread*, or *walker* into *runner*, or *cold* into *heat*.

Word Chains

☆ About the Game

This simple game may be played in a spoken or in written form.

☆ How-To's

1. In the spoken version, one player starts the game by saying any word—for example, "cat."

2. The next player has to say a word that starts with the last letter of the previous player's word. With *cat*, the last letter is *t*, so the next player might say "table."

3. The next player does the same, this time looking for a word that starts with *e*—for example, *elephant.*

4. The game continues like this. It can stop when exhaustion sets in!

5. The written version is the same, except that the words are written on a sheet of paper that is passed from player to player.

> **Skills:** Spelling skills, dictionary skills, and phonic awareness.
>
> **Players:** Pairs, groups, or whole class.
>
> **Materials:** a Dictionary and writing materials for the written version.

☆ Variation: Whole-Class Word Chains

1. Everyone in the class has a sheet of paper of the same size and writes a word on it at the same time.

2. When everyone is ready, each child passes his or her paper to the closest child. Each player writes a word starting with the last letter of the word on the sheet of paper he or she received. Then, when everyone's ready, they pass the papers on again.

3. This goes on until the players get their own sheet of paper back.

☆ Tip: These word chains can make very interesting classroom displays. Perhaps your class can invent a word chain that will go around all four walls of your classroom, or even right down the school corridor!

Word Piles

☆ About the Game

This game is as simple as can be, yet everyone loves it. Maybe that says something about simplicity!

☆ How-To's

1. Choose someone to be the Umpire, which includes being timekeeper.

2. After making sure everyone has a pencil and paper, the Umpire chooses any letter from the alphabet except *k*, *x*, *y*, or *z*. To make a random choice, the Umpire could open a book with eyes closed, touch a finger to the page, and pick the letter closest to the finger.

3. The Umpire announces the letter and starts the timer. Everyone begins to write down as many words as possible that start with that letter.

4. If players are not sure about the spelling of a word, they put a question mark after it.

5. When five minutes are up, the Umpire says "Stop!" The players now have one minute in which they can use their dictionaries to check—and, if necessary—correct the spelling of any questioned words. The first player to do this says "Finished!" The Umpire declares "Time's up!" and all the players have to stop.

6. The players now change papers with one another and use a dictionary to check that the words are spelled correctly. They write the correct spelling beside any incorrectly spelled words, then count up how many words the player spelled correctly. The total is that player's score for the game, and the child with the highest score is the winner of the round.

Skills: Spelling skills, dictionary skills, editing skills, and phonic awareness.

Players: Pairs, groups, or whole class.

Materials: Writing materials; dictionary; and a timer, watch, or clock with a second hand.

Word Stacks

☆ About the Game

This game is similar to Word Piles but has a few subtle differences. Try both—they're great spelling games and fun to play.

☆ How-To's

1. Choose an Umpire to be time manager and dispute settler.

2. The Umpire chooses a letter—any letter at all.

3. Players now have five minutes to write down as many words as possible that don't start with the chosen letter but do include it somewhere. For example, if the chosen letter is *g*, players can't use *good* or *garden* but can use *hug* or *big* or *refrigerator*.

4. Players are allowed to use dictionaries to check their spelling as they go.

5. At the end of five minutes, players exchange papers and check one another's spelling.

6. They then count up how many times the chosen letter is used in the correctly spelled words. If *g* is the letter, a word like *bigger* would score two points, while *digging* would be worth three points and *zigzagging* four!

Skills: Spelling skills, dictionary skills, editing skills, and phonic awareness.

Players: Pairs, groups, or whole class.

Materials: Writing materials; one dictionary per player; and a timer, watch, or clock with a second hand.

Telegrams

☆ About the Game

This simple game will send children scurrying to their dictionaries in search of words to complete their telegrams.

☆ How-To's

1. Select a word to start the game. One way to do this is to open a book or magazine, close your eyes, and place your finger on the page. If the nearest word to your finger has more than four letters, use it. If it doesn't, choose again.

2. Another way is to choose a word that is linked to a topic you are studying or is in some other sense significant to the class.

3. If you're really stuck, you can always choose one of the following "all rounders."

Skills: Spelling skills, dictionary skills, editing skills, and phonic awareness.

Players: Individuals, pairs, groups, or whole class.

Materials: Writing materials and a dictionary per player.

Good Telegram Words

5 letters	6 letters	7 letters	7+ letters
sport	summer	America	mathematics
earth	winter	silence	conservation
happy	people	daytime	communication
peace	animal	traffic	automobile
music	school	giraffe	television
water	friend	stories	swimming

4. The players have to use the letters from the word to make up a telegram. Their first word must start with the first letter, the second word with the second letter, and so on. Some examples follow:

> ANIMAL: A New Invention Makes Alligators Lovable
>
> WATER: Why All Tigers Enjoy Rhubarb
>
> MUSIC: Maestro's Uncle Still In Choir

5. Like ordinary telegrams, the language can be "telescoped"—that is, verbs and other words (as well as punctuation) can be left out as long as the meaning is clear. The telegram doesn't have to make too much sense because half the fun in this game is getting the writer to explain what he or she actually meant!

6. When everyone is finished, or after an agreed time limit, the telegrams are read aloud and displayed for everyone else to read.

Illustrated Idioms

☆ About the Game

This is a great opportunity for students who have some drawing ability to shine. It will also spark every child's interest in the words and expressions they use every day.

☆ How-To's

1. This game can extend over several days, enabling children to take part whenever they have spare time. For example, you might begin a game on Monday and check answers on Friday.

2. Before starting, explain that idioms are colorful expressions we use every day, such as "He ran off at the mouth" and "Her name rang a bell."

3. One player thinks of an idiom, like "It was raining cats and dogs." She or he then draws a picture depicting this literally.

4. The player puts the picture on the display board. Underneath it, pin a large, sealed envelope that you have cut a small slit in. (The slit should be long enough for a small piece of paper to fit through.)

5. The other children now try to guess the idiom. Each writes his or her guess on a slip of paper and slips it into the envelope. (With the sealed envelope, no one knows what others have guessed until the game concludes.)

6. At the end of the week (or when you decide to end the game), the envelope is opened and there is great amusement as the answers are read aloud to the class.

Skills: Idiom study, vocabulary extension, language appreciation, and cartooning skills.

Players: Large groups or whole class.

Materials: Drawing materials, display space or display board, and sealable pre-slit envelopes.

Some Weird and Wacky Idioms to Start Everyone Thinking

He bit off more than he could chew.

She completely lost her head.

She was over the moon.

He had a finger in several pies.

I have a bone to pick with you.

He thought he was the cat's pajamas.

Keep this under your hat.

He thinks he's the big cheese around here.

The cat got her tongue.

We're up the creek without a paddle.

She was on cloud nine.

Letter Collections

Letters can be written in many different ways—different sizes, different fonts, different styles. Why not start a letter collection? Encourage children to scour newspapers, and magazines to see how many different versions of the same letter they can find. Have them cut out their selections and mount them on a poster board. They might like to see how many styles they can produce with a computer, too.

Our Letter F Collection

List-O-Mania

☆ About the Game

This is a simple racing game that delivers excitement while helping to extend word fluency.

☆ How-To's

1. This list-building game requires children to think of words that have something in common. For example, the list words might all have double letters, have more than two vowels, or refer to something you find in a shopping mall.

2. Either you or the children decide on the common feature. You might have children write suggestions on pieces of paper and put them into a container. Then have a child choose one at random.

3. Set a time limit—say 10 minutes—and allow children to write as fast as they can.

4. When time's up, the players all exchange lists to check that the words follow that round's set rule and are spelled correctly. This is where the dictionaries come into play! If a word is spelled wrong, it doesn't count.

5. The winner is the player with the most words.

Skills: Vocabulary extension and spelling skills.

Players: Groups of three to six.

Materials: Writing materials and one dictionary per child.

bigger
toll
butter
ladder

tunnel
Mississippi

Squashed Words

☆ About the Game

Squashed words are made up of parts from two other words, such as *brunch* (*breakfast* and *lunch*) or the computer term *bits* (*binary* and *digits*). Lewis Carroll enjoyed making up words such as *slithy* (*slimy* and *lithe*) and *mimsy* (*miserable* and *flimsy*).

☆ How-To's

1. For the group version, divide the class into two teams.

2. Each team dreams up as many squashed words as they have members on their team.

3. Players can use the following categories to help them:

new creatures	(animals of all kinds, monsters)
new plants	(flowers, fruits, vegetables, etc.)
new gadgets	(machines, vehicles, appliances, etc.)
new recreations	(sports, hobbies, pastimes)
miscellaneous	(anything combined with anything!)

4. Each team picks a category and draws up a list of things that belong to the category. Then they choose the most unlikely pairs and see if they can make up an interesting new word by combining the first part of one word with the last part of the other. A new creature, for example, might be a cross between a dog and a centipede—a dogipede or a centipog! A new plant might be a fruit called a cabapple (a cross between a cabbage and a pineapple). A new gadget might be a spork (a cross between a spoon and a fork).

5. When the teams have decided on their creations, they write the name on one sheet of paper and draw what they think it would look like on another.

6. When both teams have finished, they exchange their papers and have fun trying to match up the words and pictures.

Skills: Word study, vocabulary extension, spelling skills, and social skills.

Players: Pairs or groups.

Materials: Paper (same-size sheets), pens or pencils, and crayons or felt pens.

Make Your Own Acronyms

Sometimes we make words out of the first letters of a number of words—for example, Scuba (Self Contained Underwater Breathing Apparatus). We also talk about UFOs (Unidentified Flying Objects), read in the newspaper about NATO (North Atlantic Treaty Organization), and take tests called SATs (Scholastic Aptitude Tests). Start your own class collection of acronyms. Then make a puzzle out of them, and see if children can guess what the letters stand for.

Perhaps your class could have some fun making up their own acronyms. For example, instead of Working In Groups children might have WIGs. You might ask children to put their work on the FAP (Finished Assignment Pile). Some of your children may not go home after school but attend an ASP (After-School Program). Any other ideas?

spoon + fork = spork

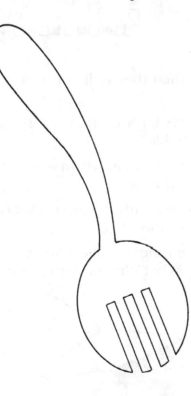

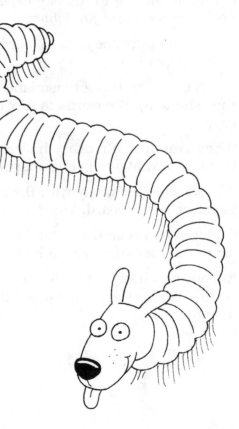

centipede + dog = centipog

Cut-Up Poetry

☆ About the Game

This may sound like mayhem with words, and in a way it is. However, it also helps children think intently about language, word by word, and maybe that is the beginning of real poetry-making.

☆ How-To's

1. Each child takes one or more pages from the newspaper and magazine supply.

2. Children cut out individual words that strike their fancy—little words like *to* and *of* and *in* and big words like *expeditious* and *querulous* and *firefighter*.

3. Each child puts the chosen words into his or her paper bag.

4. When everyone has a reasonable number, they shake up the words to mix them up. Then they pull out words one at a time.

5. When children think they have enough words for a poem, they try organizing them into whatever poetic shape seems suitable.

6. When a child is happy with the result, he or she glues them in place onto paper or posterboard. Voilà! There's a Cut-Up Poem!

7. Children can read their Cut-Up Poems to one another. The results can be very funny, or they may have a haunting mood or meaning.

8. Encourage children to talk about how these random collections of words affect them. How do the poems make them feel? What kind of thoughts do they inspire?

Skills: Language appreciation, word study, writing skills, and creativity.

Players: Individuals, pairs, or groups.

Materials: Newspapers or magazines, scissors, paper bags, glue, and posterboard or paper.

Computer Art

One of the fun things you can do with a computer is to make interesting word patterns. For example, you can take a word like *game* and write it large:

GAME

or stack the letters:

GA
ME

or make a pattern by stacking:

GAGAGAGAGAGAGAGA
MEMEMEMEMEMEMEME

or make a word-square pattern:

g a m e
a m e g
m e g a
e g a m

or change the size of some of the letters:

gAme   gAME   Game

or make a pattern by repeating it time after time after time:

Acrostic Poetry

☆ ## About the Game

Poets often play with the look of words on the page, and sometimes that shape contributes to the meaning. Acrostic poetry is one kind of visual word play.

In addition to acrostic poems and cinquains (see page 37), there are other ways to shape a poem. Your class might like to start a collection of shaped poems—both their own and those of other people. For starters, Lewis Carroll and e. e. cummings are two good sources.

☆ ## How-To's

1. Explain that poets often use visual shapes or visual tricks to help organize their poems. Acrostic poetry is one kind of trickery anyone can try.

2. Have children choose a topic and a key word that sums up that topic. You may wish to help with suggestions.

3. Children vertically write the key word down the page. Then for each letter they think of a word starting with that letter that has some connection with the subject, as in this example:

> Ghoulish
> Haunting
> Odd
> Sinister
> Terrifying
> Scream!

4. Children might also try to do the same with whole lines instead of single words:

> After everyone has gone
> Lying here on my bed
> Only sound I hear is my own breathing
> Not a soul in the whole house
> Except me.

5. Start a class collection of acrostic poems.

Skills: Word study, language appreciation, poetry writing, and spelling skills.

Players: Individuals, pairs, or groups.

Materials: Examples of shaped poems (published and perhaps your own).

Cinquains

☆ About the Game

The cinquain is a kind of poet's word game that has been around for a long time. People in medieval times liked to cinquainize, and the cinquain is probably even older than that!

☆ How-to's

1. A cinquain is a shape poem with five lines. Children make up short blank verse poems of five lines that follow certain rules.

2. Sometimes cinquain fanatics count the numbers of syllables they use in each line (which is good for encouraging syllabification skills).

3. The most common pattern is to have two syllables in the first line, four in the second line, six in the third line, eight in the fourth line, and two in the last. So a child might end up with something like this:

> Rain drops
> drip drop drip drop
> drip drop drop drip drop drop
> drop drop drop drop drip drip drip drip
> rain stops

4. A cinquain writer might concentrate on words instead of syllables. An extra word might be added to each line, like this:

> This
> is my
> first try at
> writing cinquains and I
> think I have now finished

5. Other times, a cinquain writer may focus on letters. Children can easily grasp adding an extra letter to each line like this:

> I
> go
> for
> this
> verse

6. When children have written cinquains to their heart's content, display their creations.

Word Puzzlers

☆ About the Game

Word Puzzlers are intriguing brain tweakers that involve both verbal and visual ideas.

☆ How-To's

1. Children try to express an idea by the way they write the words. Then they challenge the other players to crack the code and guess the hidden word or phrase. Here are some examples:

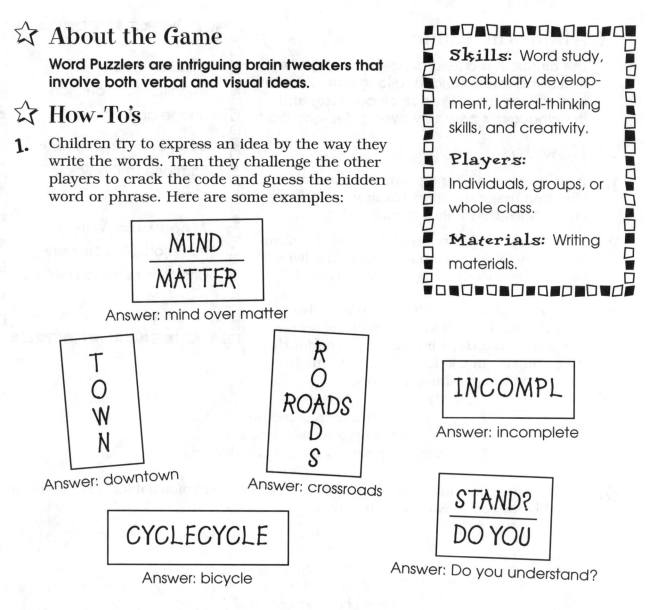

MIND
―――
MATTER

Answer: mind over matter

T O W N

Answer: downtown

R O A D S (ROADS)

Answer: crossroads

INCOMPL

Answer: incomplete

CYCLECYCLE

Answer: bicycle

STAND?
―――
DO YOU

Answer: Do you understand?

2. Children collect and invent Word Puzzlers and display them on a Word Puzzler Display Board.

3. Children try to guess what one another's Word Puzzlers really say.

☆ Extension Ideas

Start a class collection of Word Puzzlers. You might even publish them in a Word Puzzler Book. (Have the answers in the back for those who get stuck!)

Unravel a Rebus

☆ About the Game

A rebus is a story told with pictorial clues—though for this game, you may also want to use some letters and numbers. Years ago, in many parts of the world, the rebus was used as a form of written communication. Native Americans, for example, told wonderful stories with rebuses. Even the letters of the alphabet began as pictures. The letter *a*, for example, began as a simplified drawing of the head of an ox. In fact, while you're playing Unravel a Rebus, you might also encourage your class to do some research into how the alphabet came about.

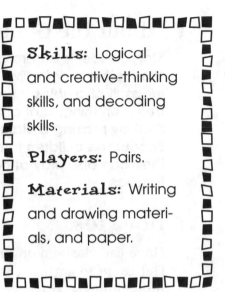

Skills: Logical and creative-thinking skills, and decoding skills.

Players: Pairs.

Materials: Writing and drawing materials, and paper.

☆ How-To's

1. Each child thinks up a story or message using a mixture of pictures, letters, numbers, symbols, and word fragments—and even (if necessary) whole words.

2. The completed rebus is written on chart paper.

3. Each child then exchanges his or her rebus with a partner and tries to work out what the message says.

4. After one or more rounds, you might feature their rebuses in a classroom display or publish them in a Class Rebus Book.

Story Builder

☆ About the Game

Story Builder is a card game that encourages children to be imaginative and experiment with ideas. It also helps them to make connections between things that at first sight seem unrelated. Start by making a class set of Story Builder Cards. Encourage children to make their own packs so they can also play at home with their friends and families.

☆ How-To's

1. Have the class go on an image hunt with you. Get them to gather a stack of magazines, shopping catalogs, travel brochures, advertisement handouts, anything that has small photos and drawings of things—from scarves and clocks to chairs and musical instruments, anything at all. The pictures just have to be small enough to fit onto your cards. Have children help you cut out the pictures and paste them on the cards. Aim for as much variety as possible. To make the cards more durable, it is a good idea to have them laminated.

2. If playing in groups, children sit around a table or in a circle on the floor. One player mixes up the cards and then deals five to each player. The players must leave the cards face down and not look at them.

3. The player to the left of the dealer now turns over his or her first card. Let's say it is a picture of a washing machine. The player must begin a story that includes a reference to a washing machine. It doesn't have to be a serious story. In fact, it is a lot more fun if the story is rather silly! For example:

   Cory: Once upon a time there was a girl called Little Red Washing Hood and she lived in a house with seven dwarfs who happened to play for the local college football team and so every Saturday they would come home from the match with all their muddy football clothes and expect poor Little Red Washing Hood to wash them—which she did—in the washing machine!

4. Now the next player turns over his or her top card. Let's say it shows a TV.

   Marcie: Poor Little Red Washing Hood! She had to sit in front of the washing machine for hours and hours waiting for the laundry to be washed. But what really upset her was that she was missing her favorite TV program!

Skills: Story-writing, thinking skills, and creativity.

Players: Pairs or groups up to eight.

Materials: Index cards, magazines, brochures, etc.

5. After that, the next player, turns over his top card, which shows a picture of a teddy bear:

> Zack: Which just happened to be a brand-new half-hour comedy called "The Teddy Bear's Picnic!"

6. The game continues until all the cards have been used. There is no scoring in this game—everyone wins by enjoying the creation of ideas.

☆ Variation: Super Story Builder

1. This is a written version. The cards are shuffled and five cards are dealt and placed face up in the middle of the group.

2. Players all have writing materials and must make up their own story involving all five objects.

3. When all have finished, players take turns reading their stories aloud.

Collect Word Trivia

Why not start a classroom collection of interesting word trivia? Here are some example:

☐ Collect words ending in *o*. There are lots of common short ones, such as *to, go, do, no, boo, zoo,* etc. Encourage children to find longer ones such as *tomato, potato, kangaroo,* and *cargo.*

■ Words ending in *u* are more of a challenge. In time, children may come up with *caribou, beau, bureau, tutu,* and a few more.

☐ Or collect palindromes—words that are spelled the same backward and forward—such as *toot, refer, Bob, Hannah, madam,* and *rotator.*

■ Find palindrome phrases such as *No lemons, no melon* or *Able was I ere I saw Elba* (perhaps uttered by Napoleon after being imprisoned on the island of Elba.)

☐ Or reversible word pairs like *bad/dab, top/pot, ward/draw, flow/wolf,* and even *repaid/diaper!*

Spelling Concentration

☆ About the Game

This game brings spelling and excitement together! Encourage children to make their own packs of Spelling Concentration Cards so that they can also play at home. If the cards don't match, it's the next player's turn.

☆ How-To's

1. Sitting around a table, the players shuffle the cards and place them face down.

2. One player begins by choosing two cards and turning them over. The aim is to find two cards that have the same words. When a pair is found, the player claims the pair and stacks them on the table in front of him or her. The player now has another turn, and continues having turns until he or she fails to get a pair. When this happens, the unmatched cards are turned over again and left in the same place. Meanwhile all players watch closely and try to memorize where the words are.

3. The next player now has a turn. Perhaps the first card is the mate of one turned over before. If the player remembers where it is, he or she turns it over and claims the pair. And so the game goes on until all the pairs of cards have been found.

4. The winner of the round is the one with the most pairs of cards.

Treasure Hunt

☆ About the Game

This is a very versatile game that can be adapted for a number of purposes.

☆ How-To's

1. Clip a number of newspaper stories that are appropriate for children. Enlarge each on the photocopy machine, and reproduce a Treasure Tally chart alongside each copy (see the sample on page 44). Beginners might look only for capital letters and periods. More competent readers and writers might also look for question marks and exclamation marks. Proficient language users might also look for commas, quotation marks, and any other punctuation.

2. Decide how much each treasure item is worth. For example, you might value capital letters at $2 and periods at $5. Keep this information secret until later in the game.

3. Set a time limit and instruct children to go searching for "treasure." They skim over the text looking for items of punctuation. Each time they find one, they draw a circle around it and put a tally mark in the appropriate column on the Treasure Tally (see page 44).

4. When time is up or when players have finished checking the passage (whichever comes first), they add up the number of treasure items in each column.

Skills: Familiarity with unctuation; skim and speed reading. The game can also develop spelling skills and a facility with prefixes and suffixes.

Players: Any number from two to the whole class.

Materials: Newspapers, writing materials, and paper.

5. Now you announce how much the items are worth, and each player works out the total value of his or her tally sheet. The player with the most valuable treasure haul is the winner of the round.

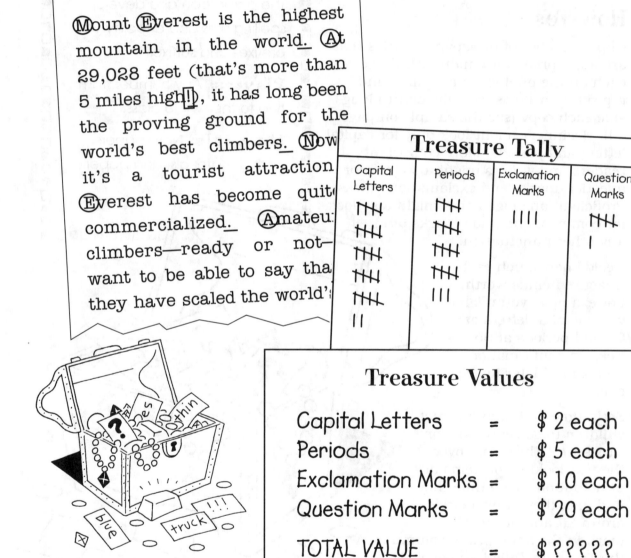

Ⓜount Ⓔverest is the highest mountain in the world._ Ⓐt 29,028 feet (that's more than 5 miles high！), it has long been the proving ground for the world's best climbers._ Ⓝow it's a tourist attraction. Ⓔverest has become quite commercialized._ Ⓐmateur climbers—ready or not— want to be able to say that they have scaled the world's

Treasure Tally

Capital Letters	Periods	Exclamation Marks	Question Marks

Treasure Values

Capital Letters	=	$ 2 each
Periods	=	$ 5 each
Exclamation Marks	=	$ 10 each
Question Marks	=	$ 20 each
TOTAL VALUE	=	$?????

☆ Variations

Use the same game format for looking for prefixes or suffixes and spelling patterns such as final *e*'s, double letters, or *ie* (as in *i* before *e*, except after *c*).

Noisy Punctuation

☆ About the Game

This is another of my favorite games! It owes something to the great musical humorist, Victor Borge, who did a wonderful sketch in which he read a passage of prose complete with audible punctuation. This game starts there but adds actions, too. It can be a great entertainment, but it also surreptitiously teaches punctuation and sentence construction. I had a class perform this game at a school concert for parents, who also joined in by performing the actions and sound effects. The result was a cacophonous and hilarious performance!

Skills: Punctuation, reading skills, and language appreciation.

Players: Whole class.

Materials: Short prose piece (preferably fiction) that is rich in punctuation marks: periods, exclamation marks, commas, question marks, etc.

☆ How-To's

1. The purpose of this game is to turn a story's printed punctuation marks into both sounds and actions. You can start with the story on the next page. Later, however, children might like to write their own noisy punctuation stories once they've gotten the hang of the game.

2. Spend some time discussing the different punctuation marks, and decide on a sound effect for each. Children might like to whistle a scale for a comma, put a finger into their mouth and make a plop sound for a period, and clap their hands for a question mark.

3. Having decided on the sound for each punctuation mark, devise a suitable action to go with it. For a comma, for example, children might like to give a deep bow. For capital letters, they might like to throw both arms into the air. A vigorous pirouette might serve to indicate an exclamation mark! Experiment and see what you can all agree on—and can all perform successfully without injuring yourselves!

4. Now comes the performance. Someone is chosen to read and conduct this "oratorio." You might place the text on an overhead projector so everyone can read it. The conductor then points to where he or she is reading, and the rest of the class performs the punctuation on cue.

THE GHOST'S NIGHT OFF!

Gertrude the Ghost was extremely tired. She had been working nonstop night after night after night.

"I'm so tired!" she told her ghostly old friend, Ms. Terry Fire. "Everyone else gets to work in the daytime, but we ghosts always have to work in the dark!"

"I know," said Ms. Terry Fire. "And people get to wear wonderful jewelry, like bracelets, necklaces, and strings of pearls. All we ghosts ever get to wear are clanky old chains!"

"Clank! Clank! Clank!" said Gertrude, as she rattled her chains.

"And being able to walk through walls is no joke," said Ms. Terry Fire. "I keep getting lost! If I'm not watching where I'm going, I find I've accidentally slipped into some-one's house or someone's bedroom and I don't know where I am!"

"I know," said Gertrude. "But the worst thing is, people are so rude to us ghosts. You go up to them and you say, 'Boo!' Of course, Boo is ghost language for 'Hello.' But does anyone ever stop and say a friendly, 'Boo,' back?"

TRY THIS!

Words for Sale!

Discuss with children the way companies try to invent brand names that will stick in our minds and help sell products. Make a collection of brand names. (Note their graphics, too—how they are written and what logos and artwork accompany them.) Your class could have fun making up its own brand names and logo designs.

What would your class call its own brand of jeans?

　　LEG-UPS　　　　PANT-ASTIC　　　COOLSTERS

What would your class call its brand of sneakers?

　　ZEBRAS!　　　　DASHERS　　　　TOE-LIMOS

Letter Race

☆ About the Game

The beauty of this game is that children often get so hooked on it that they not only play it at school but in their spare time with family and friends.

☆ How to's

1. To make the Letter Race Cards, use small index cards. You will need about 50 per pack.

2. On the cards write high-frequency or commonly used words—one word per card. Ideally, the words should all be about the same length. Have children help you. Ask them to proof one another's cards to make sure there are no spelling mistakes.

3. Have extra blank cards on hand so that when you introduce new vocabulary— say in science or social studies—you can add those words to the class Letter Race Cards. (It doesn't matter how many cards you end up with.)

4. For playing, move to an open space or gymnasium. A Wizard (in charge of "spell"ing) is chosen. He or she shuffles the cards and gives one to each player.

5. The Wizard stands near one end of the space, facing the opposite way. The others form a semicircle behind him or her, about a dozen paces away, so that each player is roughly the same distance from the Wizard. The Wizard now calls out a letter. The other players look at the word on their card. If it contains the letter, they take two steps forward (four steps if the letter occurs twice, six steps for three times, etc.).

6. When a player is close enough, he or she taps the Wizard on the shoulder. This player now become the Wizard. The cards are collected and shuffled and a new round begins.

Brain Waves

☆ About the Game

This is a great game for young writers to practice brainstorming and to start a good collection of ideas.

☆ How-To's

1. Set a time limit (say five minutes) and appoint a Timekeeper. The Timekeeper shuffles the Brain Wave Topic Cards, places them face down, turns over the top card, and reads it aloud.

2. The players immediately begin writing a list of words and phrases that have some connection with the topic. For example, if the topic is water, players might list words such as *boats*, *ocean*, *fish*, *blue*, and *rivers*.

3. When time is up, players count up how many entries (words or phrases) they wrote.

4. The player with the greatest number of entries reads his or her list aloud. If there is a word or phrase that the other players don't think has any real connection with the topic word, they can say "Challenge!" When challenged, the player has to explain convincingly (or at least imaginatively) how that word or phrase is connected with the topic.

5. If the other players are not convinced (or entertained), a vote is taken. If the majority of the players vote against the word, the player's score is reduced by one.

6. If the player loses too many words, another player may end up with more words. In that case, player number two begins to read out his or her words for the group to check. The player with the most approved words or phrases is the winner of the round and becomes the Timekeeper for the next round.

Skills: Spelling and writing.

Players: Individuals or the whole class.

Materials: Writing materials and a set of Brain Wave Topic Cards. You can make these from index cards. On each one write a different topic (see sample list below). You need about 40 to start with, but you can keep adding to them over time. Besides general topics, you might also like to use words from topics the class has studied.

Topic Words to Get Your Class's Brain Waves Flowing:

water	math	flight	cats	ocean	school
spiders	holiday	noise	lunch	dinner	books
movies	sleep	fire	shopping	rain	tired

Word Starters

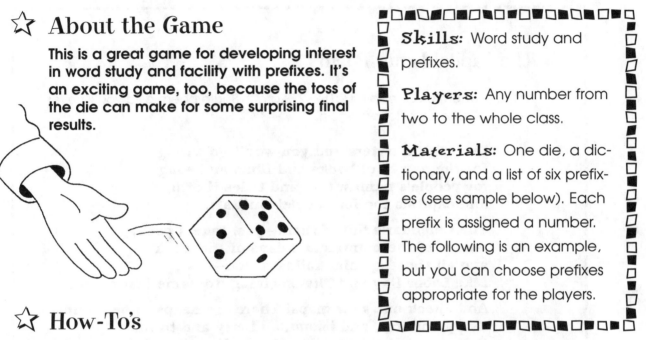

☆ About the Game

This is a great game for developing interest in word study and facility with prefixes. It's an exciting game, too, because the toss of the die can make for some surprising final results.

Skills: Word study and prefixes.

Players: Any number from two to the whole class.

Materials: One die, a dictionary, and a list of six prefixes (see sample below). Each prefix is assigned a number. The following is an example, but you can choose prefixes appropriate for the players.

☆ How-To's

1. One player is appointed Ringmaster for the first round. The Ringmaster tosses the die three times in the round. The first throw determines the prefix for the round.

1	2	3	4	5	6
pre	anti	non	de	con	im

2. The second throw determines the numbers of words that the players (including the Ringmaster) must find. Each word must start with the given prefix. When a player has written the right number of words, he or she calls out "Ready." All the other players must immediately put down their pens and pencils.

3. The Ringmaster now tosses the die again. This time the number determines how many points each correctly prefixed word is worth. Players work in pairs to check each other's spelling and also to calculate their scores. For example, if the die shows a four, then every correct word would be worth four points. A player with 6 words would have a score of 24.

4. The player with the highest score in that round becomes the Ringmaster for the next round. Players accumulate scores from each round, and the winner is the one with the highest total at the end of the game.

The Capital Letter Poem

not sure when to use capital leTTers? Learn thiS little poem aNd you'll never worry abOUt capital letters again.

> Use capital letters and you won't go wrong
> for the names of books and films and songs,
> for people's names, too, and titles if official
> and capitals too for people's initials.
>
> The Calendar's full of them—yes, take a peek,
> names of the months and days of the week
> and all those special holidays, too—
> Like Labor Day and Thanksgiving (to name just a few).
>
> And check out your maps! There are heaps to be found!
> Every country, and island, and city and town,
> the names of the plains and the rivers running through,
> every road name and street name, and avenue.
>
> And we use them in writing so our readers will see
> where our sentences start. (Thoughtful, aren't we?)
> All these capital letters, do I hear you cry?
> There's one more important one: the capital I.

— Alan Trussell-Cullen

Have a Capital Letter Hunt! Choose a story. Children try to guess how many capital letters there will be in the story. They write their guesses down (so no one can argue later) and then start counting. The one with the closest guess is declared the Capital Letter Champ!

TRY THIS!

Ghosts

☆ About the Game

This is a good game to stretch children's vocabulary. It also happens to be one of those classic word games that people of all ages have been playing for hundreds of years!

☆ How-To's

1. Let's say Mark is playing Suki, Chelsea, and Malcolm.

2. Mark starts. He thinks of the word *cross* but doesn't reveal what it is. Instead he writes just the first two letters on the chalkboard or chart paper: *c r*.

3. Suki is next, and he thinks of a word that starts with *cr*. The word he has in mind is *creep*. He, too, doesn't say anything but simply writes the next letter in the word, making *c r e*.

4. Chelsea thinks of the word *cream*, so she adds *a* as the fourth letter, making *c r e a*. The game continues like this.

5. The object of the game is to avoid completing a word. The round stops the moment someone accidentally completes a word—or can't think of another word to provide a further letter. (If they want, children can write on scrap paper to work out the words.) In this game, Malcolm may think of *creaky* and so he adds a *k*. Immediately, the other players point out that he has completed a word—*creak*—thus bringing the round to an end. (Malcolm might have thought of *create* and added *t* to make *creat*. Then back to Mark, who could have avoided finishing a word by adding *u* for *creature*. . . .)

6. Any letter added must lead to a real word. If challenged, a player must either name a possible word or choose a new letter.

7. It is fun to play the game without scoring. If you wish, however, players can earn a point for each added letter that does not complete a word.

Skills: Spelling skills, reasoning and critical-thinking skills, and word study.

Players: Groups of four to eight (which is fun) or the whole class.

Materials: Chalkboard or large sheet of chart paper (on an easel), dictionary (to help settle any disputes over the spelling of words), and writing materials so that players can try out their word ideas.

Spell-Aerobics

☆ About the Game

This variation of a spelling bee is as sweet as honey!

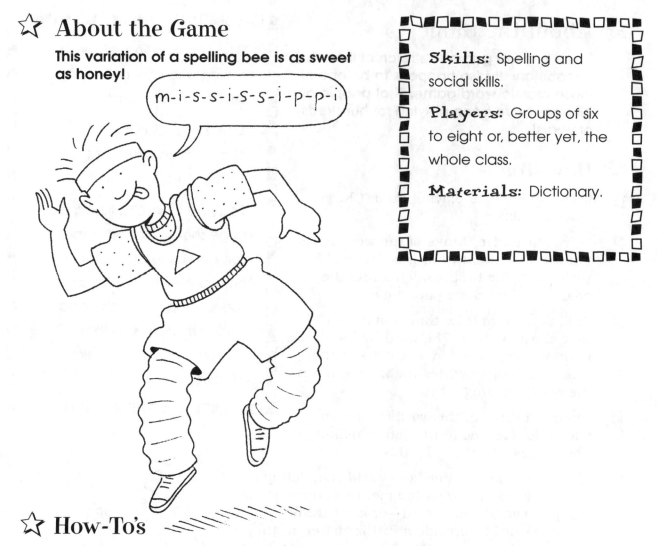

m-i-s-s-i-s-s-i-p-p-i

☆ How-To's

1. Compile a list of words that you want children to know how to spell.

2. Choose a quizmaster. The Quizmaster gets everyone to decide on certain letters that no one is allowed to say. Two letters is a good number to start with. Let's suppose the chosen letters are *i* and *s*. Instead of saying the banned letters, a suitable action is decided on for each—for example, a head scratch for *i* and a salute for *s*.

3. The Quizmaster now asks each player to spell a word.

4. Whenever the players come to the outlawed letters, they must perform the action instead of speaking. For our example with *i* and *s*, a particularly mean Quizmaster might give the players words like *dismissive* or *Mississippi*!

Alpha-Bit-at-a-Time

☆ About the Game

This is a terrific game to help children improve their spelling as they stretch their vocabulary. It's fun for children of different ages or adults and children to play together—in short, it's a great family game.

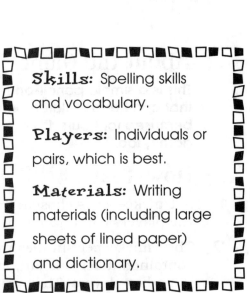

Skills: Spelling skills and vocabulary.

Players: Individuals or pairs, which is best.

Materials: Writing materials (including large sheets of lined paper) and dictionary.

☆ How-To's

1. The players write all the letters of the alphabet down the page—each letter on a different line.

2. Player One takes the paper and writes a word that contains the letter *a*—say *apple*. Players may, if they wish, check a word in the dictionary before writing it down.

3. Player Two checks that the word is spelled correctly. If so, Player One draws a circle around the letter *a*. If it is incorrect, Player Two writes a word containing *a* and then gets a second turn.

4. Player Two writes a word that contains the letter *b*—say *rub*. Player One checks it; if it is spelled correctly, Player Two draws a cross over the letter *b*. Otherwise Player One writes a *b* word and gets an extra turn. In other words, Player One circles, Player Two crosses, and so on.

5. But here's where the challenge comes in: Players do not have to use just one letter at a time. For his or her next move, Player One might write the word *credit*—and so be able to circle *c*, *d*, and *e*! And Player Two might reply with the word *thoughtful*—and thus claim *f*, *g*, and *h*. These multiple letters must all follow in sequence in the alphabet, though they may be out of sequence in the word.

6. The players continue until they have used all the letters of the alphabet. They now count the crossed letters and circled letters separately. The player with the most letters wins the round.

☆ Variation: Solo Alpha-Bit-at-a-Time

1. Children can play Alpha-bit-at-a-Time on their own, too. They work through the alphabet trying to think of words that use multiple letters. The object is to use up all the letters with as few words as possible. In this version children compete against themselves and try to better their own record.

2. Encourage children to play the solo version in their spare time. Set up a display board where they can exhibit their efforts for all to marvel at!

Word Finder

☆ About the Game

This is a simple pencil-and-paper game that can keep children amused and bemused for hours. It's a good spelling game, too.

☆ How-To's

1. A Timekeeper is chosen. (In pairs, one of the players can also be the Timekeeper.)

2. The Timekeeper shuffles the words in the container, takes one out, and spells it for the other players. They write it on their piece of paper.

3. The Timekeeper then gives the players five minutes to try to make as many words as possible using only letters from the given word.

4. The players can rearrange the letters in any order, but they must not use a letter more times than it appears in the original word. For example, if the given word is *vegetable*, the players might write *eat*, *beet*, *able*, and *table*—but not *babble* (because there is only one *b* in *vegetable*) or *ball* (because there is only one *l*).

5. The only other rules are: no foreign words, no abbreviations, and no proper nouns.

6. The winner is the player with the most words when time is up.

> **Skills:** Spelling skills, vocabulary development, and language appreciation.
>
> **Players:** Individuals, pairs, or groups of four to six.
>
> **Materials:** Writing materials and a watch (for keeping the time). Players will also need a list of suitable words, each written on a slip of paper. (Some suggestions are listed below.) Before playing, place the slips inside a container.

☆ Variation

To play by themselves, children just choose a word and see how many words they can generate from its letters. Here are some words to get you started:

measurable	atmosphere	international
undecided	multiplication	performance
disastrous	intentional	incidentally
consternation	metropolis	intelligent
destination	transportation	highway
thoughtful	accidental	photography

Mashed Potatoes

☆ About the Game

You can fit this game into almost any spare moment. So you happen to finish math a few minutes early? Time for a quick round of Mashed Potatoes. So the class is waiting for the rest of the children to arrive back from the gym? Fine time for another helping of Mashed Potatoes.

☆ How-To's

1. Two players begin—one is the Potato Masher, the other is the Cook.

2. The Cook asks the Potato Masher questions about anything at all, like "How old are you?" "Do you like ice cream?" "Is Washington the capital of the United States?"

3. The Potato Masher must answer the questions in one of three ways:

   ■ If the correct answer to the question is clearly yes (as with the question "Are you breathing?") the answer must be no!

   ☐ If the correct answer to the question is no (as with the question "Have you ever climbed Mount Everest?") the answer must be yes!

   ■ If the question doesn't have a yes-or-no answer, or if the Potato Masher doesn't know the answer, he or she must say "Mashed Potatoes!"

4. The Cook tries to trick the Potato Masher into giving the "wrong" answer and is allowed to ask up to 20 questions.

5. If the game is played in front of a group or the class, the spectators can count the questions and check that the answers are "correct."

6. If the Potato Masher makes a mistake, he or she drops out and a new Potato Masher is chosen.

7. If, however, the Potato Masher manages to answer all 20 questions "correctly," he or she becomes the Cook for the next round.

Skills: Thinking skills (reversibility) and questioning skills.

Players: Pairs or small groups. (This game works best with an audience watching.)

Materials: None.

Mystery Verbs

☆ **About the Game**

Mystery Verbs is a great game for making children more verbiferous! Okay, so that's a new word. It sort of means "mad about verbs." That's what children become when they play this game.

☆ **How-To's**

1. Before starting the game, have a discussion about verbs so that children know what they are dealing with.

2. One person is chosen to be "It" and is sent out of the room. The other children now have to choose their mystery verb, for example, *sneeze*.

3. The "It" child comes back into the room and tries to discover the mystery verb by going around the group asking questions in which the unknown word is replaced by the word *kangaroo*. For example, he or she might ask:

- Do lions in the zoo kangaroo?
- Where is the best place to kangaroo?
- Do people kangaroo?
- Do you need any special equipment to kangaroo?

4. The player can make a guess at the mystery verb at any time. If the guess is wrong, the player just keeps on asking questions.

5. Once the player guesses the mystery verb, a new "It" is chosen and the children start over with another mystery verb.

☆ **Tip:** It makes the game more fun if the children answering the questions don't just say "yes" or "no" but give some helpful, though sometimes confusing information. (They must be careful to use the word *kangaroo* instead of the real word.) For example, with *sneeze*, a player is asked, "Do you kangaroo in any special place?" He or she might reply, "Well, I sometimes kangaroo if I am in my mom's spice cupboard. And once I helped my grandma tidy up her dusty old attic and I kangarooed a lot." It also helps to brainstorm some good questions for this game. Children could write a list of questions on a chart and have it handy whenever they play the game.

6. If a player has trouble thinking up good questions, you can ask children to suggest some. With *sneeze*, for example, a helpful player might say, "Why don't you ask me: How long does it take to kangaroo?"

Fortunately ...

☆ About the Game

This is a simple game that is good for encouraging children to talk and interact. It's also good for developing reasoning and logic because the mind has to keep making 180-degree turns!

☆ How-To's

1. Players take turns telling parts of an imaginary story about something that happened to them. You (or one of the children) begin by telling an incident that involves the word *fortunately*. For example:

   > Over the weekend I decided I was going to make a cake. Fortunately, I'm a very good cook.

2. The player now points to someone else to carry on the story, but he or she has to begin with the word *unfortunately*. For example:

   > Unfortunately, I didn't have a recipe book.

3. This player chooses the next one who must continue the saga, this time with the word *fortunately*. For example:

   > Fortunately there was a bookshop down the road that sold cook books.

4. And so the game goes on, alternating *fortunately* and *unfortunately* until everyone is exhausted!

Skills: Reasoning skills, confidence, and oral language skills.

Players: Any number from two to the whole class.

Materials: None.

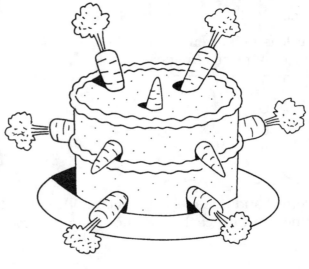

Riddle-Me-Ree

☆ About the Game

This is a very old game—the fact that people have been playing it so long is testament to its appeal. It is a cross between a writing game and a brain teaser: writing skills are coaxed along by the need to prepare the word puzzle, thinking skills by the need to solve it.

☆ How-To's

1. One person (or a small group) thinks of a mystery word and makes up a poem in which each line is a clue. The poem may be done with or without rhymes, whichever you prefer.

2. Each line (except the last) is a clue to a different letter in the word. The last line gives a clue to the whole word. For example:

   My first is in squash and also in crush.

   My second is in zoom but never in rush.

   My third is in bun but never in bread.

   My fourth is in sing but never in said.

   My last is in round but never in square.

   You never see me but you know I am there.

   (Answer: Sound)

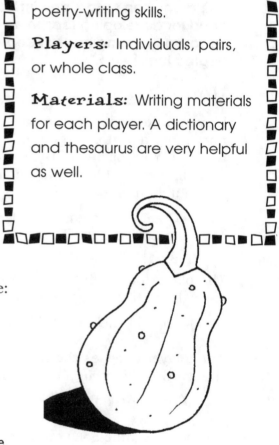

Skills: Thinking skills and poetry-writing skills.

Players: Individuals, pairs, or whole class.

Materials: Writing materials for each player. A dictionary and thesaurus are very helpful as well.

3. To start with, at least, children should choose a short mystery word. They write it vertically on a piece of paper.

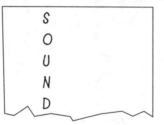

4. Then for each letter (and line of the poem), children think up two words that are vaguely connected with each other (for example, *zoom* and *rush*, or *bun*

and *bread*). The trick is that one of the words has the secret letter in it and the other doesn't.Then they make up a line using the Riddle-Me-Ree format:

> My first is in   but never in

5. Finally, they write a line giving a clue to the whole word.

> You never see me but you know I am there.

6. The finished Riddle-Me-Ree is then displayed or passed around to others so that they can try to crack the puzzle.

☆ **Extension:** You might set up a Riddle-Me-Ree Display Board, or have children store their creations on the class computer. You can also prepare your own class Riddle-Me-Ree Puzzle Book.

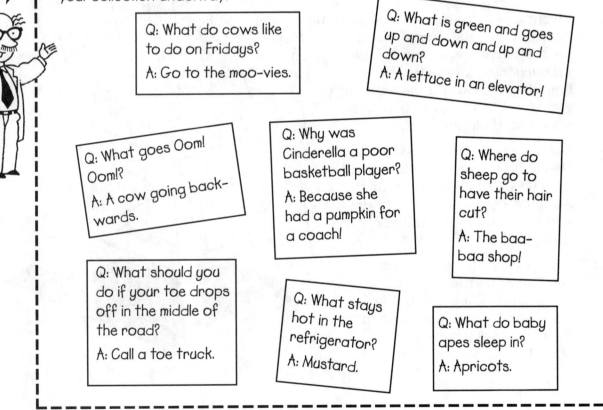

A Griddle of Riddles

Ordinary riddles are great word games in their own right. Why not start a Class Riddle Collection? You might like to publish it in the form of a Class Riddle Book. Encourage children to keep their own riddle collections, too. Here are some riddles to help get your collection underway:

Q: What do cows like to do on Fridays?
A: Go to the moo-vies.

Q: What is green and goes up and down and up and down?
A: A lettuce in an elevator!

Q: What goes Oom! Oom!?
A: A cow going backwards.

Q: Why was Cinderella a poor basketball player?
A: Because she had a pumpkin for a coach!

Q: Where do sheep go to have their hair cut?
A: The baa-baa shop!

Q: What should you do if your toe drops off in the middle of the road?
A: Call a toe truck.

Q: What stays hot in the refrigerator?
A: Mustard.

Q: What do baby apes sleep in?
A: Apricots.

New Names for Old

☆ About the Game

With this game, children begin seeing familiar objects in new (and sometimes wacky) ways—and scramble for words to describe them.

☆ How-To's

1. Choose an everyday object like a chair. With the help of the group or the class, make a list of things you can do with it.

- ■ Sit on it.
- ☐ Use it for putting things on.
- ■ Stand on it when *you* want to reach high things.
- ☐ Use it for making holes in the garden so *you* can plant four seeds at a time!

2. Invent a new name for it—something offbeat that is based on at least one of those uses. Maybe it's a *sit-upon*, or a *down-plonker*, or an *upreacher*, or a *uni-stepladder*, or, if you sit back to front on it, a *horsette*, or if you use it in the garden, a *quad-speed seed planter*.

3. Draw a plan of the classroom. Divide it into sections, and divide the class into groups of four to six. Assign a section to each group, and have children rename everything in their section!

4. Create your own Classroom Dictionary featuring all these new names, providing a suitable definition (perhaps accompanied by a drawing) for each.

Skills: Vocabulary building, language appreciation, and creative-thinking skills.

Players: Any number from two to the whole class.

Mateials: Writing materials and an everyday object (for the introduction).

Collectibles

☆ About the Game

This is another of my favorite games. Mathematicians will tell you it helps children to organize information in sets—and to name those sets. Linguists will tell you it introduces children to collective nouns. Poets will tell you it encourages children to experiment with language. Try it yourself and see what you think.

☆ How-To's

1. Divide the class into two groups. Each group has a large sheet of paper on which they write the headings "Animals," "Objects," and "People's Roles." These should be well spaced across the full width of the paper (See chart below.)

2. The groups now brainstorm plural nouns for each heading. They write the nouns on the paper, leaving a space in front of each one. Their lists should start out looking something like this:

Skills: Grammar skills (collective nouns), creative-thinking, and language appreciation.

Players: Individuals, groups, or whole class.

Materials: Writing materials and a few large sheets of paper. (Since the game is all about collective nouns, it is a good idea to introduce lots of them a day or so before you actually try out the game.)

Animals	Objects	People's Roles
ants	teaspoons	babies
butterflies	bath plugs	swimmers
kangaroos	potatoes	clowns

3. Each team stops when it has a total of 25 plural nouns. When both groups are ready, the teams exchange lists.

4. Now team members put their heads together and try to dream up an interesting and unusual collective noun for each item. Some examples follow:

Animals	Objects	People's Roles
an obedience of ants	a clatter of teaspoons	a babble of babies
a flutter of butterflies	a gurgle of bath plugs	a splash of swimmers
a hoppity of kangaroos	a mash of potatoes	a chuckle of clowns

5. It sometimes helps to set a time limit—say ten minutes. After that, the teams share their ideas. Allow time for children to savor each word creation.

☆ **Extra tips:** This game is addictive, and some people (like me) love to play it on their own. Start a class collection of collectibles and display them for everyone to see. Who knows? Some children's original ideas may be so catchy that people everywhere will start to use them.

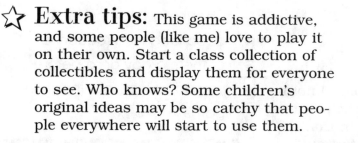

Terrific Titles

☆ About the Game

Children have double fun with this activity—thinking up their own Terrific Titles and enjoying everyone else's.

☆ How-To's

1. The aim of this activity is to come up with imaginary book titles and author's names that together make punning jokes. The book covers below give a better idea than any description.

2. Have the class collect and/or invent as many such titles as they can. Keep the collection on a display board, and encourage children to continue adding new ones.

Skills: Language appreciation, creative-thinking skill, and puns.

Players: Any number from one to the whole class.

Materials: Writing materials.

Some examples to start your collection:

A SHOCKING TALE
by
Electra Fide

AMAZING IDEAS
by
Ida Brainstorm

PREHISTORIC REPTILES
by
Terry Dactyl

GETTING RICH QUICK
by
Robin Banks

A TRIP TO THE DENTIST
by
Phil McAvity

Fictionary

☆ About the Game

This is a wonderful game. It is quite challenging, but once the mechanics and dynamics have been mastered just about everyone can enjoy playing it—children and adults. Not only is it entertaining but it also encourages children to concentrate and to appreciate nuances of meaning. Fictionary also requires players to be both imaginative and convincing! A simplified version is added for younger children.

☆ How-To's

1. Before introducing the game you might encourage children to study some dictionary definitions so they have some feel for the style and format required.

2. One player is chosen to be the Fictionarian—let's say it is Peter.

3. Peter opens the dictionary at random and looks for a word that he thinks the other players will not know. He picks the word *gunny*. Peter tells the players the word and spells it for them, so they can write it down.

4. They now make up a dictionary definition for the word. They try to make it sound so convincing that others will think it is the right meaning. They write down their definition on a piece of paper, making sure no one else sees it. They also write their name.

5. Peter writes two definitions. On one piece of paper he writes the main definition from the dictionary, **gunny:** *coarse sacking or sack usually made from jute fiber.*

6. On another piece of paper Peter writes his own made-up definition, for example: **gunny:** *small green tropical fish able to swim backward.*

7. Peter collects all the definitions and shuffles them well, along with the two he wrote. He numbers them consecutively.

8. Peter now conceals the papers behind a book or clipboard so that the players cannot recognize them. He reads each definition aloud, along with its number. He must not give any clues as to which is which.

Skills: Dictionary usage, language appreciation, vocabulary development, creative-thinking and social skills.

Players: Any number from three to twelve.

Materials: Writing materials and scratch paper for each player, and a good general-purpose, adult dictionary (not a children's dictionary).

9. The other players decide which definition seems most convincing. Then they write down its number.

10. After allowing the players a couple of minutes to make up their minds, Peter calls out the numbers again. Players put up their hands when he comes to the number of the definition they chose. Peter counts the number of votes and writes it on the definition paper.

11. Peter now reads the definitions again, naming the author of each fake definition (including his own). The number of people who chose that definition becomes that player's score.

12. Players who chose the correct definition score two extra points. For the next round, the role of Fictionarian passes to either the round winner or the child sitting next to the first Fictionarian.

gunny: coarse sacking or sack usually made from jute fiber.

Dictionary

☆ Simplified Version

1. You choose the words and make up three or four fake definitions for each one. (Your colleagues may enjoy contributing some!)

2. Read out the real and fake definitions of one word. Repeat them as many times as necessary.

3. Children guess which is the correct definition. (This could be done orally, if you wish.)

4. Children check their dictionaries to see which definition is correct.

Cats and Dogs

☆ About the Game

People have been playing this game for at least 200 years in one form or another. Besides being an exciting game—the tension rising as you get closer and closer to that final answer!—it's challenging in so many ways.

☆ How-To's

1. One player is chosen to start the game. Let's say Jackie is going to start with a group of friends.

2. She chooses a four-letter word and writes it down on a piece of paper, taking care no one sees it. The word is *game*. On a larger sheet of paper, so all can see, she draws a grid with six columns (see next page), and marks four x's at the top to stand for the four letters of the mystery word. At the top of the two columns to the right she either draws a cat and a dog or writes the letters *c* and *d*.

3. The other players try to guess the mystery word, and Jackie gives them clues as they go.

4. One player guesses the word *show*.

5. Jackie writes the word *show* and checks to see if there are any correct letters in the right place. Those would be dogs, but there are none. Now she looks to see if there are any correct letters in the wrong place. Those would be cats, but there are none of those either. So she writes a zero in both the cat and dog columns.

6. Now a player volunteers the word *milk*. Jackie writes this in the grid and then checks it. The *m* is a correct letter in the wrong place, so she scores one cat and no dogs.

Skills: Reasoning, deductive logic, hypothesizing, categorizing, spelling and social skills.

Players: Pairs, groups of three to ten, or whole class.

Materials: Writing materials, large sheet of paper, chart paper, or the chalkboard.

7. And so the game continues, with the players suggesting four-letter words and Shannon giving them clues by indicating how many cats and dogs. After a while, children will learn to pick words that keep dog letters in the same position and have cat letters in different positions. Here are the results of Jackie's game.

X	X	X	X	CATS	DOGS
S	H	O	W	0	0
M	I	L	K	1	0
S	W	I	M	1	0
T	I	M	E	0	2
S	A	M	E	0	3
G	A	M	E	0	4

☆ **Variation:** Once children have mastered the game, have them try words of five, six, or even seven letters.

Categories

☆ About the Game

This popular game has been around for more than a hundred years. Proof of its appeal can be seen in the many commercial imitations on the market. Because it involves the use of reference tools, it's an excellent game to play in the library or media center.

☆ How-To's

1. Before playing the game, you will need to prepare a pack of category cards. You might enlist children's help. Begin with a discussion of categories, using headings such as:

    - Geography (names of countries, lakes, rivers, mountains, etc.)
    - Nature (names of plants, vegetables, fruits, trees, insects, animals)
    - People (names of boys, girls, languages, occupations, etc.)
    - The Solar System (names of planets, heavenly bodies, stars, etc.)

2. You will need about 40 cards, but you can add new ones later. (It is a good idea to add categories that relate to topics you are studying.) Write each category on a separate file card.

3. Players begin the game by drawing a chart like the one on the next page. To start with you might choose six columns and six rows. In the top left box write *Letter*. Players shuffle their packs of cards and turn over the top five to find their categories. Now players enter them in the boxes at the top of each of the remaining columns.

4. Select five letters. For each letter, you might have a child close his or her eyes and plunge a finger into the middle of a book page, choosing the nearest letter. Ask them to write the letters in the first column.

5. The players try to fill in the grid with words that belong in the category and start with the letter in the first column.

6. Categories and letters can be chosen the same way when children play in pairs or teams. When playing by themselves, however, children can choose whatever categories and letters they like.

Skills: Categorizing information; using reference tools such as dictionaries, atlases, and encyclopedias; vocabulary extension; and spelling.

Players: Individuals, pairs, or whole class.

Materials: Writing materials, blank index cards; and a range of reference tools such as an atlas, almanac, dictionary, thesaurus, and encyclopedia.

X	NAME	CITY	ANIMALS	FRUITS & VEGGIES
P	Paul	Philadelphia	porcupine	peach
R	Rebecca	Rome	rooster	raspberry
A	Andrew	Antwerp	ant	apple
L	Leslie	Los Angeles	lynx	lettuce
T	Tanya	Toronto	tiger	tangerine

☆ **Variation:** You could post a Categories Challenge of the Day for children to work on when they have some spare time. At the end of the day, see how many have managed to finish it. Applaud any unusual or surprising choices.

Famous Folks

☆ About the Game

Playing this game helps to stretch children's word power and imagination.

☆ How-To's

1. Players take turns reaching into the container and drawing out a name. Each player writes down what his or her famous person likes to eat. We're not talking reality here—the player must come up with a "food" that follows these rules: it consists of an adjective that begins with the first letter of the first word of the person's name and a noun that begins with the first letter of the second word. For example, if the name is Marco Polo, the food might be Mashed Potatoes!

2. When all players have their answers ready, they sit in a circle and ask the first player "Who are you?"

> A: Marco Polo.
>
> Q: And what do you like to eat, Marco Polo?
>
> A: Mashed Potatoes!

The children now ask the next player And who are you? The answer might be "Donald Duck."

> Q: And what do you like to eat, Donald Duck?
>
> A: Delicious Dates!

Of course, famous people don't always eat sensible things:

> Q: And who are you?
>
> A: Miss Muffet.
>
> Q: And what do you like to eat, Miss Muffet?
>
> A: Minced Mouse!

Skills: Phonic awareness, spelling skills, grammar (adjectives and nouns), and dictionary skills.

Players: Pairs, groups of four or five, or whole class.

Materials: Writing materials and a dictionary. You will need a collection of names of "famous folks"—not only real people of past and present but also fictional characters from books or movies. They should be two-word names such as Abraham Lincoln, Tom Hanks, or Porky Pig. Write these on cards and put them in a box or container.

☆ **CLASSROOM TIP:** You might like to start a class Adjective Store to help children play this game. Make a chart with the alphabet written vertically down the left side, and let the children see how many good (or silly!) adjectives they can come up with for each. It's a fun homework assignment, too. Give children some letters to work on, and suggest that they ask their families to help!

APT AND AUDACIOUS ADJECTIVES WE CAN USE
WHEN PLAYING FAMOUS FOLK

A   acrimonious, archaic, antique
B   beauteous, botched, belligerent
C   colorful, clotted, creative
D   dubious, delirious, doleful
E   enormous, expensive, excruciating
F   famous, fatuous, frisky
     . . .and so on.

Aunt Tilly

☆ About the Game

This game can be maddening for anyone who has never encountered it before. (That's why it's such fun for those who *do* know how to play!) It sounds utterly irrational, and yet it's an excellent game for developing reasoning skills.

☆ How-To's

1. One player begins by telling everyone about Aunt Tilly, as in this example:

> Aunt Tilly likes pepper but she doesn't like salt.
>
> She loves coffee but she hates tea.
>
> She likes sleeping but she hates going to bed.

2. The other players try to get more clues about Aunt Tilly by asking questions such as "Does Aunt Tilly like soup?"

3. The first player may reply, "Oh no, she hates soup. But she loves eating anything with a spoon."

4. Behind all the apparent nonsense is a secret code that the player decided on in advance. In this example, the code is that Aunt Tilly likes words that contain a double letter. But it could be words that contain a particular letter, or start with a vowel, or contain a final silent *e*, or consist of two syllables, or have anything else to do with letters or syllables.

5. As players decipher the code, they join in and assist the first player. You may wish to set a time limit. If not, the game ends when everyone has guessed the code or those who haven't give up.

Skills: Thinking skills (ability to reason and use logic), spelling skills (including syllabification), and social skills.

Players: Five to ten players is best, but can also be played with the whole class.

Materials: None.